COUNTRIES IN OUR WORLD

UNITED
KINGDOM
IN OUR WORLD

Michael Burgan

A⁺
Smart Apple Media

Published by Smart Apple Media
P.O. Box 3263, Mankato, Minnesota 56002

Printed in the United States of America at Corporate
Graphics, in North Mankato, Minnesota.

Published by arrangement with the Watts Publishing
Group LTD, London.

Library of Congress Cataloging-in-Publication Data
Burgan, Michael.
  United Kingdom in our world / by Michael Burgan.
    p. cm. -- (Countries in our world)
  Includes bibliographical references and index.
  Summary: "Describes the geography, landscape,
economy, government, and culture of the United
Kingdom today and discusses the UK's influence of
and relations with the rest of the world"--Provided by
publisher.
  ISBN 978-1-59920-435-2 (library binding)
 1. Great Britain--Juvenile literature. 2. Northern
Ireland--Juvenile literature. I. Title.
  DA27.5.B875 2012
  941--dc22
                          2010035508

1305
3-2011

9 8 7 6 5 4 3 2 1

Produced for Franklin Watts by
White-Thomson Publishing Ltd
Series consultant: Rob Bowden
Editor: Sonya Newland
Designer: Amy Sparks
Picture researcher: Sonya Newland

Picture Credits
Corbis: 6 (Kevin Coombs/Reuters), 7 (Gideon
Mendel), 10 (Brian Stewart/epa), 11 (Bryn
Colton/Assignments Photographers), 12 (Gideon
Mendel), 14 (Howard Davies), 15 (Nik Wheeler),
19 (Antoine Gyori), 23 (Tony West), 24 (Andy
Rain/epa), 26 (Toby Melville/Reuters), 28 (Ashley
Cooper); **Dreamstime:** 5 (Diademimages), 8 (Apw),
17 (Valeria Cantone), 20 (Stephen Finn); **Fotolia:**
18 (Sam Shapiro); **iStock:** 21 (Ann Taylor-Hughes);
Photolibrary: Cover (Eric Nathan); **Shutterstock:** 9
(Chris Pole), 13 (Jenny Solomon), 16 (Kevin Eaves),
22 (Photogl), 25 (Angelina Dimitrova), 29 (Tadeusz
Ibrom); **ISAF Media:** 27 (Sergeant James Elmer).

Contents

The United Kingdom is one of the most developed countries in the world. Although small in size, it once controlled an empire that included a quarter of the world's land and people. Today, the country has only a few overseas colonies, but its global influence remains strong.

Where in the World?

The United Kingdom is an island off the northwestern coast of mainland Europe. It is made up of four countries: England, Scotland, Wales, and Northern Ireland. These are ruled by a central government in the English capital, London, however each country has some power of self-rule. Apart from the land border between Northern Ireland and the independent Republic of Ireland, the UK is surrounded by water.

Nations Coming Together

The United Kingdom rose out of the growing strength of England. During the 13th century, English armies defeated those in neighboring Wales.

▲ The UK is surrounded by the North Sea, the English Channel, the Atlantic Ocean, and the Irish Sea. Its closest neighbors on the continent of Europe are France, Norway, and the Netherlands.

The English tried to take over Scotland as well, but the Scottish resisted. The two kingdoms finally united peacefully in 1707 under the name Great Britain. The British also controlled Ireland, and when the Irish gained independence in 1921, Northern Ireland remained part of the United Kingdom.

IT'S A FACT!

The term United Kingdom refers to England, Scotland, Wales, and Northern Ireland. The name Great Britain only includes England, Scotland, and Wales. The British Isles is the name given to Great Britain, Ireland, and other smaller islands, such as the Channel Islands of Guernsey and Jersey.

A World Power

Throughout its history, the UK has had far-reaching connections with other countries. Over the centuries, the British gained control of many distant lands and eventually ruled a vast empire. Ships brought natural resources from faraway places, and British factories turned those materials into goods that were sold around the world. British people also settled in the colonies, taking with them their language, art, religions, and customs. This helped British culture spread throughout the world. Although virtually all the colonies are now independent, many of them have kept cultural and political ties with the UK.

▼ *The UK has a central government based at the Houses of Parliament in London, but Scotland, Wales, and Northern Ireland also have their own national governments.*

International Relations

The United Kingdom remains close to most of its former colonies and dominions. Many of them belong to the Commonwealth of Nations, an organization formed by the UK in 1931. Its members work together to promote shared goals around the world, such as democracy, equal rights, free trade, and world peace. The United States is one of the UK's closest allies, and the two nations fought together during World War I (1914–18) and World War II (1939–45). Today, they are major trading partners and have joined forces in the War on Terror, focused in the Middle East and Central Asia. Other nations are also helping in this struggle.

GOING GLOBAL

The English language is one of the UK's greatest exports. Today, more than 40 nations use it as their official language, and about 350 million people speak it as their first language. Experts estimate that around one billion people are currently learning English.

▼ *U.S. president Barack Obama and British prime minister Gordon Brown. The UK and the U.S. have close political ties.*

▲ *The UK's multicultural society has developed from years of immigration, particularly since the end of World War II.*

BASIC DATA

Official name: The United Kingdom of Great Britain and Northern Ireland

Capital: London

Size: 94,058 sq miles (243,610 sq km)

Population: 61,113,205 (2010 est.)

Currency: Pound

Looking Ahead

Despite its wealth, the UK faces some tough challenges. The population is expected to grow by about six million people by 2020 partly because of the large numbers of immigrants settling in the UK. They will need education, jobs, and services such as healthcare, and the government will need to find ways of paying for these. Therefore not everyone in the UK welcomes immigrants, fearing they will take away jobs and housing.

The government hopes to provide for everyone's needs and end any tension between the immigrants and citizens. The UK is also facing competition in selling its goods and services in global markets, especially from countries such as China and India, which are developing strong economies. Government officials hope that by promoting education and new ideas in science and technology, the UK can continue to be a global influence.

Landscapes and Environment

Almost completely surrounded by water, the United Kingdom is made up of hundreds of islands. The biggest, Great Britain, covers 88,795 sq miles (229,979 sq km) and is the eighth-largest island in the world. Island groups off the coast include the Shetlands, Orkneys, and Hebrides.

Highlands and Hills

A large part of the UK is covered with hills and low mountains. The Scottish Highlands, to the north, are home to Ben Nevis, the UK's highest peak at 4,406 feet (1,343 m). The Southern Uplands stretch to the border with England, which is marked by the Cheviot Hills. The Pennines, another range of hills, run from north to south across the border, reaching into central England and forming a kind of backbone through the central UK. The country's hills and mountains continue into Wales where the Cambrians are the main mountain range. Northern Ireland also has several small mountain ranges. Rocky cliffs dot the coastline all around the country.

PLACE IN THE WORLD

Total area: **94,058 sq miles (243,610 sq km)**

Percentage of world land area: **0.16%**

World ranking: **79th**

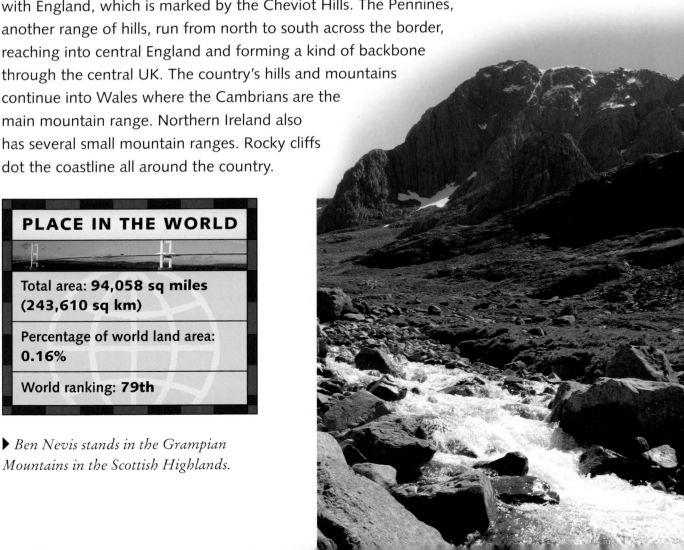

▶ *Ben Nevis stands in the Grampian Mountains in the Scottish Highlands.*

Pastures and Meadows

The heart of England is much flatter than the lands to the west and north. Rolling hills covered with pastures and meadows circle many cities and towns, and some more isolated areas are covered in moorland. The damp land of many moors supports a variety of grasses and small plants.

 The Severn Bridge connects England and Wales where they are separated by the River Severn.

Rivers and Lakes

Rivers flow through all parts of the United Kingdom. The longest is the River Severn at 220 miles (354 km). It starts in the Cambrian Mountains and flows west into the Bristol Channel. To the east, the Thames flows from Gloucestershire to the North Sea— a distance of 211 miles (340 km). Other important rivers include the Trent and the Great Ouse. The Lake District, in northwest England, is famous for its beautiful landscapes and is a popular tourist destination. There, 14 main lakes and many smaller ones lie among mountains up to 3,200 ft. (975 m) high. The UK's largest freshwater lake, Lough Neagh, lies in the middle of Northern Ireland.

IT'S A FACT!

The world's oldest insect fossil was discovered in Scotland in 1919. This ancient insect was fossilized in rock about 400 million years ago, although only parts of its jaw remain. The fossil is now owned by London's Natural History Museum.

Climate

The climate is temperate in the UK, which means that the temperature does not usually drop sharply in winter or soar in summer. The warm ocean waters of the Gulf Stream help keep the islands relatively warm and free of snow during most winters. In summer, sea breezes keep the country cool. In January London has an average high temperature of 44°F (7°C). In July, the average high is 73°F (23°C). In general, temperatures are highest in the south and coolest in the Highlands of Scotland. Rainfall is high all over the UK, thoguh the west coast gets more rain than the east. London has an average rainfall of 23 inches (59 cm) per year.

GOING GLOBAL

The Giant's Causeway in Northern Ireland is one of the UK's best-known World Heritage Sites—places selected by the international organization UNESCO for their natural beauty or their cultural and historical significance. The causeway consists of lava remains that flowed about 60 million years ago. There are about 40,000 stone columns grouped closely together along the shore. Rapid cooling of the lava shaped most of the stones into six-sided columns, although some have more or fewer sides.

▼ *Rainfall is high in the UK. In 2009, record rainfall levels caused floods in northern England.*

Environmental Issues

Like many countries, the UK faces several environmental issues. Cars and factories cause air pollution, and waste from factories is polluting the waters. The UK has taken several steps towards addressing environmental problems, though. It has met the targets set by the international Kyoto agreement to reduce greenhouse-gas emissions, but there is still much work to be done in tackling pollution and climate change.

Wildlife

Hundreds of animal species make their homes in the UK's waterways and sea shores, including otters, various reptiles and amphibians, and sea birds. The country's forests and fields also have a great variety of wildlife, including deer, foxes, rabbits,

▲ *Programs to clean up the UK's waterways have resulted in otters and other wildlife returning to the Thames.*

THE HOME OF...

The Scottish Crossbill

Crossbills—birds of the finch family—can be found in many countries, but in 2006 scientists announced that one species is unique to Scotland. Unlike related species, the Scottish crossbill has a distinct call used to attract a mate. Scientists have called this the bird's "Scottish accent."

wildcats, and bats. There is only one species of poisonous snake in the UK—the adder. This is the only snake native to Scotland.

Since its days as a global empire, the UK has attracted people from other nations. Today, immigrants from India, Pakistan, and many other former colonies contribute to the UK's diverse population.

Who Are the British?

Just over 90 percent of Britons are white. Most people are of English descent, followed by Scottish, Welsh, and Northern Irish. Black people and Indians each make up about two percent of the population. Pakistanis make up 1.3 percent. The remaining Britons are of mixed background or other ethnic origin.

▼ *At school, children are taught about different religions and cultural backgrounds.*

GOING GLOBAL

In 2007, the following countries outside the European Union (EU) provided the most new settlers to the United Kingdom:

India	14,865	Zimbabwe	4,280
Pakistan	10,825	Nepal	4,155
Philippines	8,485	Nigeria	3,965
Iraq	7,020	China	3,440
South Africa	5,805	Bangladesh	3,330

PLACE IN THE WORLD

Population: **61,113,205 (2010 est.)**

Percentage of world total: **0.88%**

World ranking: **22rd**

Where Do They Live?

England has the largest population of the four countries in the UK with more than 51 million inhabitants. Most live in the central and eastern regions, particularly in and around the largest cities: London, Birmingham, Leeds, Sheffield, Bradford, Liverpool, and Manchester. Scotland has just over 5 million people, most centered around its capital, Edinburgh, and the second-largest city, Glasgow. The population of Wales is around 3 million, while Northern Ireland has about 1.8 million people.

Population Growth

Across the UK, a rise in the number of births and a decrease in deaths means that the population is rising rapidly. The population increase is also helped by net migration as more people enter the country from abroad than leave to live in other countries. In 1997, net migration was less than 50,000 people; in 2007, it was more than 200,000.

▲ *Birmingham is the second-largest city in the UK with a population of nearly one million.*

Newcomers to the UK

People from other countries in the European Union are allowed to settle freely in the UK. Since 2004, more than 10 countries have joined the EU, and many residents of these nations decided to move to the UK, especially those from Eastern Europe. Tens of thousands of people came from Poland, and several thousand arrived from Bulgaria and Romania. Others choosing to live in the UK are refugees fleeing wars or other troubles in countries such as Iraq, Afghanistan, Somalia, and Zimbabwe.

Immigration Issues

The ongoing rise in immigration has sparked a population boom in some towns. Sometimes there is not enough money to provide public services for the newcomers, and schools struggle to teach foreign-born students who speak little or no English. On the other hand, many adult immigrants arrive with college educations and established professions. The challenge for these people is trying to find jobs that match their skills.

IT'S A FACT!

In 2009, a record number of international immigrants applied for citizenship in the United Kingdom. About 220,000 people were granted UK passports.

◀ *This boy fled with his family from the war in Iraq. He attends evening classes at a special school that teaches refugee children in their own language.*

▲ *There are large communities of Britons in countries such as Spain. Some people emigrate when they retire, but others just want a more relaxed lifestyle.*

Moving within the UK

Many people move around within the borders of the UK. Throughout the 20th century, hundreds of thousands of people in Scotland and northern England moved south to look for work in cities such as London. However, in 2007 almost 250,000 people left London to live in other parts of the country. This reflects a new pattern of city dwellers moving to suburbs or even rural areas far from the cities. They seek more space or want to avoid the crime often found in cities. Technology, such as the Internet, also means that many jobs can be done outside the cities—even from home—giving people more freedom in choosing where to live.

GOING GLOBAL

Some UK residents choose to move overseas. Although some leave for a short time and then return to their native country, others never return. In 2007, about 340,000 British people migrated to other countries, down from a record high the year before. Popular destinations for emigrants include the United States, Germany, Spain, Australia, and Canada.

Culture and Lifestyles

For thousands of years, British culture has been influenced by the different backgrounds of the people who have settled there. More recently, British writers, artists, and musicians have created works that are world-famous.

A Range of Influences

More than 10,000 years ago, settlers came to the British Isles from Europe. In the centuries that followed, the Celts, Romans, different Germanic tribes, and other Europeans followed. All brought their own languages, shaping the English that is spoken today. In parts of Scotland, Wales, and Northern Ireland, some people still speak languages with Celtic roots.

A Religious People

For centuries, most people in the UK were Roman Catholics, but in the 16th century the Protestant Church of England became the main religion. Today, Britons follow a variety of Christian faiths, but immigrants from Asia, the Middle East, and Africa have brought other religions to the UK, including Islam, Hinduism, and Buddhism.

▼ *Hundreds of old churches, such as this one in Underbarrow, Cumbria, still stand in villages all over the UK.*

▲ *Bagpipers play at the opening of the Highland Games on the Scottish island of Skye.*

A Music-Loving People

The cultural variety of the UK is reflected in its music. Folk musicians play songs that are hundreds of years old, and Scotland's famous Highland Games often feature bagpipes. Classical composers, such as George Frederic Handel and Benjamin Britten, wrote music that is still performed all over the world. Pop groups, such as the Beatles and the Rolling Stones, also gained a worldwide following. Some British musicians combine modern styles with the music of their homelands. M.I.A., a singer-songwriter with family roots in Sri Lanka, blends hip-hop and South Asian styles. Her music is enjoyed around the world.

FAMOUS BRITONS

George Frederic Handel
1685–1759

George Frederic Handel was born in Germany. He first came to London in 1710. A few years later, Handel began to write music for King George I, another German by birth. Handel eventually settled in England. His musical works are still played and enjoyed around the world, especially the *Messiah*. This piece about the life of Christ is often played before Christmas or Easter.

Educated and Informed

England is home to two of the world's best universities, Cambridge and Oxford. Although most people can read and write, in general, the school education system is not considered as strong as that in many other European countries. The government-owned British Broadcasting Company (BBC) offers radio and television programs across the UK, as well as a news website. The BBC is also a major global player in the media, and its television programs and radio service are transmitted worldwide. Hundreds of private companies also offer radio and television services, and daily newspapers are published across the country.

GOING GLOBAL

Since 1932, the BBC World Service has provided news to dozens of countries around the world. At first only available on radio, the World Service now also offers Internet news in 33 languages, including Russian, Chinese, Swahili, and French.

▼ *Founded in the 12th century, Oxford University is one of the oldest—and one of the best—in the world.*

Sports

The modern forms of several sports were born in the UK, including soccer, rugby, golf, table tennis, and cricket. English soccer players are known and respected all over the world, and many of them play for soccer clubs in other countries where they are in much demand. Athletes from the UK have also performed well at the Olympics. London hosted the 1948 Summer Games, and more than 200 countries will send athletes to the 2012 Games, which will again take place in London.

▲ *This young rugby fan has painted his face as the English flag, a red cross on a white background.*

Art and Entertainment

More than 400 years ago, William Shakespeare wrote plays featuring comedy, romance, and history. Today, he is read more often in English-speaking nations than any other writer. Since his time, Britons have continued to write books, plays, and poems that are enjoyed around the world. Such classic tales as *Frankenstein, Robinson Crusoe,* and *The Lord of the Rings* were written in the UK. In painting, J. M. W. Turner, Thomas Gainsborough, and Francis Bacon are among internationally famous Britons.

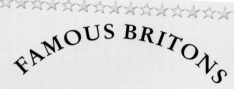

FAMOUS BRITONS

J. K. Rowling
b. 1965

In 1996, J. K. Rowling published a fantasy story about Harry Potter, a boy studying to become a wizard, and later added six more books to the series. She has become one of the most successful modern writers, selling hundreds of millions of books around the world. Several films based on the *Harry Potter* series rank among the most popular of all time.

Economy and Trade

Over the centuries, trade with other countries helped make the UK one of the wealthiest nations in the world. Although hit hard by the economic crisis that began in 2008, with valuable resources and skilled workers it is still the world's sixth-largest economy.

PLACE IN THE WORLD

Value of economy: **US$2,787 billion**

Percentage of world total: **4.5%**

World ranking: **6th**

Goods and Services

British factories produce goods that are exported all over the world, including vehicles and medicines. London is a global center for another kind of industry—banking and financial services. Many international financial companies have their European headquarters in "the City" of London. In insurance, Lloyd's of London is world famous, doing business in more than 200 countries. There has recently been a move away from manufacturing, with financial companies and other service industries employing about 80 percent of the UK's workers.

▼ *The City, an area of just 1 square mile (2.5 sq km), is London's main financial district.*

Farming

British farm and fishing products help feed people around the world. Industrialized farming allows just 2 percent of the population to grow 60 percent of the country's food. Top food exports include grains and meat products. However, the UK relies on other nations for some of its food, importing such goods as beverages, fruits, vegetables, and fish.

Natural Resources

Oil found beneath the North Sea and the goods made from it are some of the UK's major exports, and natural gas is another North Sea resource. BP, based in London, is one of the world's largest energy companies. It searches the world for new sources of oil and natural gas. The UK also has large amounts of coal and other natural resources such as tin and limestone.

▲ *Livestock farming is an important part of the UK economy, as meat products are a major export.*

IT STARTED HERE

The Industrial Revolution

England was the birthplace of the Industrial Revolution. During the 1760s and 1770s, James Watt perfected a steam engine that powered equipment used to make textiles. Steam power and machines made it easier to produce a variety of goods more quickly and cheaply than ever, and their use spread around the world.

Tourism

Tourism is an important part of the UK economy, and the country attracts visitors from around the world. Almost 30 million foreign tourists visited the UK in 2010, and they spent more than US$25 million. The foreign travelers and tourists from within the UK make tourism one of the country's major industries. More than 2.5 million people work in jobs tied to tourism.

IT'S A FACT!

The euro is the unit of currency for most EU nations. The UK, however, has chosen to keep its own currency, the pound. Denmark is the only other EU member that is not currently using the euro or planning to adopt it.

◀ *London is the UK's top tourist destination. Visitors enjoy the city's many historical sites as well as modern attractions, such as the London Eye.*

Renewable Energy

The Industrial Revolution led to the vast use of oil, coal, and natural gas as sources of power, and this meant that too much of these precious resources were used up. As reserves declined—and people realized the harm caused to the environment by burning them—production fell. The government now promotes the use of renewable sources of energy, such as wind and water power. The UK ranks eighth in the world in terms of wind power. Marine Current Turbines of Bristol, England, is a world leader in building turbines to capture the energy produced by tides and ocean currents. However, the UK still falls behind many other nations in terms of total power generated by renewable resources. Its climate means it cannot harness solar power as much as sunnier countries, such as the United States or those in the Mediterranean.

▲ *The UK already has several wind farms, and there are plans to build the world's largest offshore wind farm off the coast of southeast England.*

Trade Partners

The United States is the UK's major trading partner. In 2008, the UK sent goods worth more than US$52 billion to America, while receiving goods valued at just over US$38 billion. Other top trading partners are Germany, France, the Netherlands, and China. To promote a healthy world economy, the UK belongs to several international organizations. The Group of Eight (G8) hosts meetings between the leaders of the world's most powerful industrial nations. The Group of 20 includes nations that are quickly expanding their economies. The UK hosted a G20 meeting in 2009.

FAMOUS BRITONS

Sir Richard Branson
b. 1950

Richard Branson began his business career producing and selling music. He called his company the Virgin Group, and it soon expanded into many other areas. Today, the company has 50,000 employees in 29 countries. Now a billionaire, Branson has given some of his wealth to international charities. He was knighted in 1999.

Government and Politics

The United Kingdom is a constitutional monarchy, which means that although the queen is the head of state, the country is governed by the prime minister and parliament. Across the UK, the people choose who serves in parliament and on local councils.

The Monarchy

For centuries, monarchs were the supreme rulers of England, Scotland, and Wales. Over time, citizens gained a say in how the country should be run by electing members of parliament. By the end of the 17th century, parliament had greater legal powers than the monarch. Despite this, the monarch remains an important symbol for the UK, and continues to be ruler of the Commonwealth states such as Australia.

▼ *Prince Charles is heir to the throne of the UK and the countries of the Commonwealth.*

FAMOUS BRITONS

Prince Charles
b. 1948

Prince Charles, eldest son of Queen Elizabeth II and Prince Philip, is next in line to the throne of the UK. He is known for his work with several charities and his interest in environmental issues. In 2007, Prince Charles started the Rainforests Project to stop the cutting down of trees in the world's tropical rainforests.

Parliament

Parliament is divided into two parts called houses. The House of Commons has 646 members, who are elected by voters. There are around 750 members of the House of Lords, who are mostly appointed by the monarch. Some hold their seats for life, while others can pass their seats on to their children when they die. Scotland has its own parliament, while Wales and Northern Ireland have assemblies. Each of these bodies passes laws for its particular region. Local governments, called councils, handle such issues as education, road repair, and maintaining public spaces.

IT'S A FACT!

In 1215, English nobles forced King John to sign a document called the Magna Carta. In this, the king promised to protect some of the nobles' rights and gave them more power than they had ever had before. The Magna Carta is considered one of the world's most important documents in the creation of modern democratic government.

▼ *The Scottish parliament, established in 1998, is based in the capital Edinburgh.*

Parties and the Prime Minister

Most members of parliament and local leaders belong to political parties. The largest in the UK are the Conservatives, the Labour Party, and the Liberal Democrats. The party with the most elected members in the House of Commons chooses the leader of the government, called the prime minister. The prime minister chooses other ministers to head different government departments. These departments handle such issues as defense, protecting the environment, and foreign affairs. Many countries that were once part of the British Empire use a similar parliamentary government. These include India, Barbados, and Malaysia.

GLOBAL LEADER

Tackling Climate Change

Around the world, fears of global warming are high. The burning of fossil fuels and other human activity add to the rising temperature. In 2009, British prime minister Gordon Brown called for other industrial nations to join the UK in increasing efforts to reduce global warming. He said that by 2050, these nations should cut their emission of the gases that cause global warming in half.

◀ *No. 10 Downing Street contains the home and offices of the British prime minister. Here, Gordon Brown greets the president of Pakistan and his daughter.*

IT'S A FACT!

As one of the permanent members of the United Nations (UN), the UK can veto, or overturn, any resolution passed by the council. In recent decades, the UK has used this power only a few times.

▲ *British troops are still stationed in Afghanistan to help bring stability to the region.*

The United Nations

As a world leader, the UK plays an important role in several international organizations. The UK was one of the founding members of the United Nations, which today has almost 200 members. The British hold one of five permanent seats on the UN's most powerful body, the Security Council. The council actively tries to end disputes between member nations and keep peace around the world.

Military Power

The UK is 1 of about 10 countries with nuclear weapons, although it has never used them in battle. Instead, it relies on its army, navy, and air force for defense. The UK—along with 27 other countries—is a member of the North Atlantic Treaty Organization (NATO). This group's original goal was to defend Europe and North America from invasion. Now at times, NATO sends troops around the world. As part of NATO, the UK has sent thousands of soldiers to Afghanistan to help fight the "War on Terror." The UK also supported the U.S. invasion of Iraq in 2003.

Environmental issues, an aging population, and the rise in immigrant numbers are just some of the issues the UK will face in the near future. However, the government and the British people are already taking steps to address these situations.

Going Green

The current push to "go green" will change how Britons get their energy. There are proposals for the government to pay homeowners who use wind and solar power to generate their own electricity. All homes will also have new meters that measure how much power is used. People will know right away if they are using more power than usual so they can look for ways to cut back. The government will need to work hard to make sure the country is greener in the future.

Still a World Leader?

In the years ahead, skilled researchers in many industries could help the UK strengthen its economy. Several medical centers and universities are seeking to slow the effects of aging, fight cancer, and reduce the risk of heart disease and other deadly illnesses. New drugs and medical techniques could save lives and create jobs. However, it may take time to recover from the economic problems of the first decade of the 2000s.

▼ *There are already eco-villages such as BedZED in the UK, and in the future, there may be more green communities.*

▲ *The Notting Hill Carnival celebrates the UK's cultural diversity. More immigration in the future will enhance the country's multicultural nature.*

FAMOUS BRITONS

John Taylor, Lord Taylor of Warwick b. 1952

The son of immigrants from Jamaica, John Taylor was a successful lawyer and politician in 1996 when he received surprising news—he was about to become the first black member of the House of Lords. He hopes to use his lifelong seat to help other British blacks fight racism and succeed in the United Kingdom.

A Changing Population

As the population of the UK ages, it will also become more diverse. The number of non-white Britons has risen steadily since 2001, and some cities will have more non-white residents than whites by the 2020s. Non-whites, however, are not well represented in parliament. The major parties seek to have a more diverse government in the years to come. Attitudes and ideas from people of many backgrounds will help the UK face the challenges of the future.

Glossary

colony a territory under the immediate political control of a state.

democracy a type of government where people vote for thsoe they wish to represent them.

economy the financial system of a country or region, including how much money is made from the production and sale of goods and services.

emigration when someone leaves the country of their birth to settle in another country.

emissions gases that are given off during industrial processes or by vehicles.

ethnic group a group of people classed together according to their racial, national, linguistic, or cultural origin or background.

export to send or transport products or materials abroad for sale or trade.

fossil fuels fuels made from the remains of plants and animals that died millions of years ago; coal, oil, and natural gas are all fossil fuels.

global warming the gradual rise in temperatures on the surface of the earth caused by changes in the amount of greenhouse gases in the atmosphere.

greenhouse gas a gas that helps trap warmth in the atmosphere, which can contribute to global warming if too much is generated on earth.

immigrant a person who has moved to another country to live.

import to bring in goods or materials from a foreign country for sale.

moor an open, grassy area, often covered with marshes.

nuclear weapons bombs and other explosive weapons that get their power from nuclear reactions.

pollution ruining the environment with man-made waste or garbage.

refugee someone who flees from war, oppression, or persecution in search of refuge and safety.

resources things that are available to use, often to help develop a country's industry and economy; resources could be minerals, workers (labor), or water.

rural relating to the countryside.

suburbs areas on the outskirts of cities that are less built-up than city centers.

terrorist a person who uses violence or causes fear to try to change a political system or policy.

textiles cloth or fabric, usually made from weaving or knitting.

Further Information

Books

The United Kingdom Today
Today
by Michael Gallagher
(Sea-to-Sea Publications, 2009)

A Visit to the United Kingdom
Today
by Rachael Bell
(Heinemann Library, 2008)

Focus on the United Kingdom
World in Focus
by Alex Woolf
(World Almanac Library, 2007)

United Kingdom
by Rachel Bean
(National Geographic, 2007)

England
Exploring Countries
by Walter Simmons
(Bellwether Media, 2010)

Web Sites

**https://www.cia.gov/library/publications/
the-world-factbook/geos/UK.html**
CIA World Factbook – United Kingdom. Includes a
map and current statistics on the United Kingdom and
its people.

**http://news.bbc.co.uk/2/hi/europe/country_
profiles/1038758.stm**
The BBC offers facts on the country and links to recent
news stories from the country.

http://www.statistics.gov.uk/hub/index.html
For the latest national and local statistics on
population, economics, and more.

*Every effort has been made by the publisher to ensure
that these web sites contain no inappropriate or offensive
material. However, because of the nature of the Internet,
it is impossible to guarantee that the contents of these sites
will not be altered. We strongly advise that Internet access
is supervised by a responsible adult.*

Index

Numbers in **bold** indicate pictures